# Leaping Lion Cubs

Growing Up Wild

Madison Parker

Norwood House Press

**Cataloging-in-Publication Data**

Names: Parker, Madison.
Title: Leaping lion cubs / Madison Parker.
Description: Buffalo, NY : Norwood House Press, 2026. | Series: Growing up wild | Includes glossary and index.
Identifiers: ISBN 9781978574083 (pbk.) | ISBN 9781978574090 (library bound) | ISBN 9781978574106 (ebook)
Subjects: LCSH: Lion--Infancy--Juvenile literature. | Lion--Juvenile literature.
Classification: LCC QL737. C23 P375 2026 | DDC 599.757--dc23

Published in 2026 by
**Norwood House Press**
2544 Clinton Street
Buffalo, NY 14224


Designer: Rhea Magaro
Editor: Kim Thompson

Photo credits: Cover, p. 1 Theodore Mattas/Shutterstock.com; p. 5 Jamen Percy/Shutterstock.com; p. 6 Anan Kaewkhammul/Shutterstock.com; p. 7 Henk Boggard/Shutterstock.com; pp. 8, 9 Richard Juilliart/Shutterstock.com; p. 10 Stu Porter/Shutterstock.com; pp. 11, 16 L Galbraith/Shutterstock.com; p. 13 Maggy Meyer/Shutterstock.com; p. 14 Sheril Kannoth/Shutterstock.com; p. 15 ruek66/Shutterstock.com; p. 17 oNabby/Shutterstock.com; p. 18 Dr. Ajay Kumar Simngh/Shutterstock.com;p. 19 Micheal Potter II/Shutterstock.com; p. 21 nwsph/Shutterstock.com;



Printed in the United States of America

# TABLE OF CONTENTS

# Leaping Lion Cubs

Lions grow up in the **wild**.

Baby lions are called cubs.

# How Lion Cubs Look

Lion cubs are born with fur.

They are **blind** for the first week after they are born.

Lion cubs have short ears.

They have **whiskers**.

Lion cubs have four paws.

They have long tails.

# How Lion Cubs Sound

Lion cubs live in family groups. They meow to **communicate** with other lions.

Cubs purr when they want **affection**.

They growl to give a warning.

## What Lion Cubs Eat

Cubs drink their mothers' milk for the first few months.

Lions eat meat. They are **carnivores**. At first, cubs are confused by the taste of meat.

Cubs soon learn to like meat. They eat what is left of the adults' kills.

# Lots to Learn

Cubs stay with their mother after they are born.

When they are about two months old, cubs meet the rest of the **pride**.

Lion cubs learn by **imitating** other lions. They leap and play.

Cubs pretend to fight and hunt.

They **stalk** and pounce.

## All Grown Up

By the time they are four years old, young lions are **mature**. Adult males leave the pride. Adult females stay.

# Glossary

**affection** (uh-FEK-shuhn): love and care

**blind** (blinde): unable to see

**carnivores** (KAHR-nuh-vorz): animals that eat only meat

**communicate** (kuh-MYOO-ni-kate): to share information and feelings

**imitating** (IM-i-tay-ting): copying what others do

**mature** (muh-CHOOR): fully grown or developed; adult

**pride** (pride): a group of lions that live together

**stalk** (stawk): to move quietly and carefully, often to follow or hunt something

**whiskers** (WIS-kurz): long, stiff, sensitive hairs that grow near a cat's mouth

**wild** (wilde): natural places where no people live

# Thinking Questions

1. What are baby lions called?
2. When do lion cubs meet the rest of the pride?
3. What do lion cubs learn to do?
4. How do lion cubs communicate?
5. What happens to adult male and female lions?

# Index



# About the Author

**Madison Parker** spent her childhood in the city of Chicago, Illinois. A farm girl at heart, today she lives in Wisconsin with her husband and four children on a small farm with cows, goats, chickens, and two miniature horses named Harley and David. Her favorite dessert is vanilla frozen custard with rainbow sprinkles, even in the winter.